Ann—
Heres [...] patching holes in your Bucket List.

IS THERE A
HOLE
IN YOUR
BUCKET LIST?

Marilyn Sherman
4/24/19

Also by Marilyn Sherman

Whose Comfort Zone Are You In?

Why Settle For The Balcony? How To Get A Front-Row Seat In Life!

Front-Row Service

What People are Saying About
Is There a Hole in Your Bucket List?

"Great read. This book helps you determine what holds you back and makes sure that the goals you are pursuing are really what YOU want."
– *Linda Swindling, JD,*
Author of Ask Outrageously; The Secret to Getting What You Really Want.

"Marilyn has a way of sharing her ideas that are easy to read and understand. I'm a big fan a having a bucket list, and I hope after reading this book others will too!"
– *Laurie Guest,*
CSP Guest Enterprises, INC

"Inspiring, hopeful and most of all an enjoyable vision of how to live a better life, "Is There a Hole in your Bucket List" reminded me to dream big and believe in myself. Everyone needs to be reminded that walking in gratitude will take them so much farther than sitting in whatever emotion or belief holds them in place, and your voice sings just the right notes to lead the way! Brava!"
– *Dana Babel,*
District Manager of a Global Contract Service Solutions Company

Tired of waiting for tomorrow to go for it and reach your dreams? This book will help you go big or go home, so you can fill your bucket list full of the life you want to live. Inspiring, powerful, and easy to read, this book is like a dear friend who's got your back - and who won't let you make any excuses for not going for your biggest dreams.
– *Phil Gerbyshak,*
Digital Sales Expert

"Marilyn's latest book will inspire you to do more with the one life you have. She challenges readers to pay attention to what really matters, and overcome any doubts and fears you might have in achieving your best life. Read this book, have fun creating a list and even more fun enjoying crossing life goals off your list.."
– *Neen James,*
Keynote Speaker and Author of Attention Pays

"The disappointment of missed goals and broken promises can make us wonder what kind of person we truly are. It is so refreshing to read this powerful book on how to accept ourselves for what and who we are, reaching higher for the bucket list fulfillment, and realizing that we can make all of our dreams come true by embracing what makes us unique. Fantastic book by my friend and one of my favorite speakers, Marilyn Sherman."

– Jason Hewlett, CSP,
CPAE Speaker Hall of Fame, Author, Keynote Speaker, Entertainer

"Marilyn Sherman has written an excellent guide for attaining the level of a life well-lived. As I was told time and time again by my dear elders: You can't benefit from experiences you aren't having. Go out and work on that bucket list. Marilyn shows you how to start and how to avoid the quicksand of doubt, fear, and other traps. As the philosopher Seneca said; Nothing of value can be learned while sitting."

– Tim Durkin,
President, Seneca Leadership Programs

"Sometimes putting ourselves first seems like something for later. Marilyn walks us through a process that allows for later to happen now."

– Jess Pettitt,
Social Justice professional

"Like Having Coffee with your Best Friend. Even if you are not a fan of self-help books, this is an insightfully-written, plain-language analysis of what we all go through at different times in our lives and an amazingly enjoyable read! I felt like Marilyn was sitting and talking with me about our lives and loves; definitely a keeper."

– Maria O'Connor,
Partner at Tropicasa Real Estate

"This book is a powerful reminder to set big goals and eliminate excuses so you can reach your dreams!"

– Rita B. Craig, SHRM-SCP,
President Top Tier Leadership

Special Acknowledgments

There are a lot of people I'd like to acknowledge for helping me complete this book. I had an idea and then Karyn Buxman, and Greg Godek quickly encouraged my writing retreat and supported me with a doable, albeit aggressive, schedule. Val Hanke and her son Austin were the perfect hosts for me as I used their beautiful home in Coronado, California as a retreat to write. Thank you!

Thank you to my clients who hire me and end up becoming amazing friends: Dana Babel, Jill Prout, Beverly Carmichael, Holly Harris, Joyce Gilbert, Stephanie Luros-Gilbert, Judy Irwin, Gabe Hosler-Lancaster and Clarice Turner.

I have amazing friends and colleagues in the speaking world who gave me feedback, comments, ideas, and suggestions along the way. A special thank you to Colette Carlson, Linda Swindling, Pamela Jett, Neen James, Mark LeBlanc, Rita Craig, Sylvie di Guisto, Tim Durkin, Phil Gerbyshak, Judi Moreo, Patricia Fripp, Phil Reinhardt, Joel Block, Theresa Rose and Bill Stainton. Thank you Bonnie Davis for all the work you do behind the scenes for me.

Thank you to all the contributors who permitted me to use their stories and their experiences in this book: Stacy Sherman, Jason Hewlett, Chérie Roe, Angela Gaffney, Manley Feinberg, Mark Jackson, Ruth Hall, John Polish, and Kirsty Spraggon. I also want to acknowledge people who followed my Bucket List Marathon and contributed their ideas of what's on their bucket lists: Eric Dodge, Barbara Horan, Sheryl Greenblatt, Patrick Maurer, Mary C. Kelly, Lynn Enck Nelson, Valerie Tucker, Betsy Allen-Manning, Sunnie Glasier, Allen Klein, Marla Laughlin, Steven Iwersen, Roland Thomson, Kelli Swanson Jaecks, Lea Haben Woodford, Patti Pokorchak, Mary Patterson-Furlan, Traci Brown, Lisa Brathwaite, Carolyn Hinds, and Karen Jacobsen.

Then there are those people that just support me in their friendship, faith, and mentorship or all of the above: Nido Qubein, Maria O'Connor, Jane Atkinson, Lori Wilkinson, Bea van der Voort, Michael Hoffman,

Connie Podesta, Margie Schroeder and Randall Hinds.

Finally, some people went above and beyond what I asked for, and I'm not sure I could repay what they did for me. If you were to create a list of attributes that would make up a Friendship Bucket List, these two would probably possess many of those traits. Jess Pettitt and Susan Young, you are the ultimate in friends who give without keeping score. Thank you for your brilliance!

IS THERE A HOLE

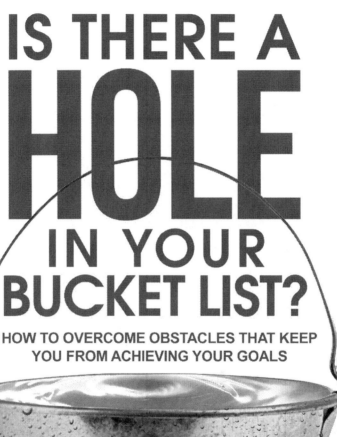

IN YOUR BUCKET LIST?

HOW TO OVERCOME OBSTACLES THAT KEEP YOU FROM ACHIEVING YOUR GOALS

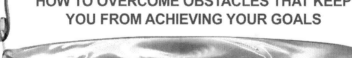

Desires
Aspiration
Goals
Vision Dreams Hope

MARILYN SHERMAN, CSP

Is There a Hole in Your Bucket List?

How to overcome fear and other obstacles that prevent you from fulfilling your dreams.

Marilyn Sherman, CSP

UpFront Presentations

Helping People Get A Front-Row Seat In Life!

9030 W. Sahara Ave #444

Las Vegas, NV 89117

702-631-5700 – Marilyn@MarilynSherman.com

Is There A Hole In Your Bucket List?

Copyright @ 2017 by Marilyn Sherman, CSP

CSP™ stands for Certified Speaking Professional. The CSP designation is conferred by the National Speakers Association and is the highest earned international measure of professional platform competence. Less than 12 percent of the speakers worldwide hold this designation.

ISBN#: 978-0-9666139-2-6

Cover design by Ryan Lause

First Printing September 2017

Printed in the United States of America

To My Frenchie –

You are the best part of my bucket list.

Contents

Chapter 1
The Bucket in the Beginning

~

*"When something is important enough, you do
it even if the odds are not in your favor."*
– Elon Musk

~

Chapter 1

The Bucket in the Beginning

Why did I write this book and what does it mean?

Most people know what a bucket list is. From the moment *The Bucket List* hit the movie theaters in 2007, the phrase has been part of our everyday vernacular.

In fact, when you mention a cool vacation you went on or a special game you attended, people get excited and say "Oh, that's on my bucket list!" In fact, I recently met a woman who lives in Wisconsin and my husband asked her how she liked living through those winters. He then said, "Ice fishing is on my bucket list." I've been married to this man for almost 12 years and I've never heard these words come out of his mouth.

When people say, "That's on my bucket list," it's a shorter way of saying, "I would really love to do that one day or see that one day before I die." Or, "That is such a dream come true for me, I mean I've dreamed of that my whole life." When you hear, "That's on my bucket list." There is no need to explain anything more. You know that you are talking about something special to that person.

When I ask different people what's on their bucket list, I've never had someone say, "What's that?" I've also never had anyone say, "Nothing." Once in awhile, I'll hear someone say, "I don't have a bucket list I'm too busy doing things." Whether you see a bucket list as a list of dreams to fulfill before you die, or as your goal list on steroids, it really doesn't matter. What matters is, if you have a bucket list, you don't sabotage that list with things that derail your efforts.

Jack Nicholson and Morgan Freeman were directed by Rob Reiner in the Bucket List movie, about two men who had been diagnosed with inoperable cancer and shared the same hospital room. Jack Nicholson's character became curious when he saw what his roommate was writing. He was writing a list. It was Freeman's bucket list of what he wanted to do before he died. It was a great movie because Jack Nicholson's character had seemingly unlimited funds, so the movie was about them going on the adventure of a lifetime in a private plane, crossing things off their bucket list! What I love about the movie, aside from it getting more and more people thinking about writing their own bucket list, are the items they had on their list.

1. See something majestic
2. Laugh until you cry
3. Kiss the most beautiful girl in the world

These items changed the way I saw a bucket list. My view of what was important and attainable was expanded and I became more sensitive to what's important to other people.

However, this book isn't about writing and creating your bucket list. This book is for people who already have a bucket list and are struggling to check things off of it. Maybe they *are* working their way through their bucket list, but there is one thing that they just can't seem to grasp, or they get a piece of it and let it go. Perhaps it falls through, or they fall just short of their goal. That brings me to why I wrote this book.

I've always been a goal setter, growing up as I did in a family of visionaries. Dad would frequently sit down with the kids and ask "Where do you see yourself next week, next year, or five years, 10 years from now? What are your tombstone goals, write them down let's discuss." So, I've always written down goals and strived to achieve them.

1. Become a barrel racer. (It's a sport with horses, what a blast!) *Check*
2. Become a paid professional speaker (for over 22 years so far) *Check*
3. Visit the Eiffel Tower ….yes, and I married a Frenchman to make sure I see her often! *Check*
4. Write a motivational best-seller …working on it.
5. Live in Las Vegas - Yup. Current place of residence. *Check*

My dad wasn't the only one who inspired me to set goals and follow my dreams. My mom was also a visionary who owned a company called Visions International. She instilled in me the idea that I could do anything that I put my mind to. She believed in having a vision and creating reality out of that vision.

Because of their support, I grew up with the habit of writing down goals, dreams, aspirations and then find a way to work toward them. Then, when I achieved them, I get to celebrate big time! I have to say it is a massive thrill to be able to say a goal was accomplished. It's actually a rush to cross something off of my to-do list, so crossing something off my goal list or bucket list is extremely exciting! Every time I accomplish a goal, especially one where there is a hurdle I have to overcome, or a naysayer that I want to prove wrong, it feels amazing. My biggest thrills are when I hear from people who have seen one of my keynote speeches and they tell me how they were able to overcome their fears to accomplish their dreams and goals.

Why did I write this book, then? Well, there is one thing that has always eluded me and that was to lose weight, and keep it off. I know, a lot of people struggle with losing weight and I am not alone. But, I have lost and gained 30-35 lbs more often than I'd like to admit. When my father died, I was grieving and mourning, as would anyone who had just lost someone close to them. I just couldn't focus on my weight goals as I went about my life with him not in it. After a while, though, I noticed that my clothes weren't fitting and I was tired, lethargic, and didn't feel like myself. I know that I was in denial about how much weight I had gained, because I had stopped weighing myself. I knew I needed to make a decision to stop the erratic eating and feeling shameful guilt at gaining the weight yet again. I got on the scale a year almost to the day my dad died. There was the number: I had gained 32 lbs in one year! I'm not blaming the weight gain on my dad's death, I'm just using the dates as a milestone. When I saw that number, I asked myself "Why do I always do this to myself? Why do I keep putting holes in my bucket list?" That's how the title of this book you are now holding came to be; from my own experience of sabotaging my own success. I had a vision of my list of dreams being literally inside of a bucket. That bucket held my hopes and dreams, my visions and aspirations. Yes, my bucket (dear Liza) had a hole in it, and my dreams were pouring out of that hole. Remember that song from your childhood? "There's a hole in my bucket dear Liza, dear Liza. Then fix it dear Henry dear Henry fix it!" The song is very catchy and goes 'round and 'round. When I had the realization that I was sabotaging my success, my brain connected that song with my bucket list and I came up with the title of my book.

Once I told people my concept, they loved it. They identified with it and I knew I was on to something. I knew I couldn't be the only one who writes out the same goal every single year, even though I repeatedly fell short. I can't be the only one who has success in one area of my life, while still struggling with another. Yet, I don't give up. I don't want you to either.

From my own journey, as well as that of the thousands of other people who get tripped up on their path to success, I have put together ideas of hope and inspiration to patch the holes in our buckets once and for all. Picture your list of dreams no longer falling through the holes in your bucket created by fear and doubt, old pain and frustration, shame, and negativity. Let's take action to patch those holes with hope, strength, power, and trust.

I know what you may be thinking: you've tried kicking this bad habit before. You've tried losing weight, stopping smoking, saving money for that bucket-list trip of a lifetime, and you fell short. You don't have *time* to accomplish what's on your list. You're busy. You're taking care of other people, or maybe you're paralyzed by fear or insecurity or lack of confidence. So what? Now's the time to re-commit, re-energize, re-organize, and re-engage in fulfilling your lifelong dreams. Let go of the fear - or whatever it is that's holding you back - and go for it!

In order to see if there is a hole in your bucket list, let's first take a look at your list. There are no rules to your bucket list. There is no set length; it can be short or long. Whatever you say it is, is right. Your bucket list is flexible and fluid too. What you write today may be different than what you've written before, or what you may write next year or even next week. If you already have a bucket list, take it out now and look at it, or re-write it here. If you don't yet have a bucket list, now's the time to write one.

To give you some inspiration, I've solicited some friends to share some items on their bucket lists. Some of these have been accomplished, some have not..yet!

Traveled to Europe by myself for an extended one-way trip
– *Patti Pokorchak*

Learned how to ride a motorcycle
– *Mary Patterson-Furlan*

Swim with the sharks!
– *Traci Brown*

Attend Abergavenny Food Festival in Wales
– *Lisa Brathwaite*

Fish in Alaska – *Carolyn Hinds*

Have my memoir turned into a lifetime movie
– *Connie Pheiff*

Perform at the Sydney Opera House
– *Karen Jacobsen*

See the Northern Lights – *Eric Dodge*

Visit Gorillas in their habitat.
– *Barbara Horan*

Visit every cavern in the U.S.
– *Sheryl Greenblatt*

Overcame my fear of heights and bungee jumped and skydived!
– *Patrick Maurer*

Fly on and off a U.S. Carrier – *Mary C. Kelly*

Visit Mt. Rushmore – *Lynn Enck Nelson*

Try out for a play – *Valerie Tucker*

Storm chase – *Betsy Allen-Manning*

Complete an Ironman, repeat Boston Marathon
– Sunnie Glasier

Have a NY Times Best-Seller *– Allen Klein*

Around the world vacation *– Marla Laughlin*

Learn to speak *fluent* French *– yes, that one is mine*

To get a bigger bucket! *– Steven Iwersen*

Heaven *– Roland Thomson*

Some people responded with a more detailed story of what was on their bucket list:

I served, networked and campaigned to become the President of The American Dental Hygienists' Association 2014-15.
– Kelli Swanson Jaecks

In 2011 I lost the right side of my face to Lentigo Maligna and lost my media job. I went through several surgeries, and skin grafts, to put me back together. I put myself through film school in 2014 and now have a National TV show.
– Lea Haben Woodford

I've survived Malignant Breast Cancer Twice, so each year I mark off 2 bucket list items.
– Ruth Hall

As far as stories go, my dear friend Laurie Guest shared her take on her bucket list. She calls it a 'life list' so that she would start working on it now instead of someday. She also solicited help from a family member:

"My niece Lauren is one of the people I love most in the world, and she also maintains a life list. Seeing the Oprah Winfrey Show live is one of the items that appeared on both of our lists. When

8

we heard that 2011 would be the last year the Oprah Winfrey Show would air, we knew the odds of getting tickets were slim. Instead of being discouraged, we compromised by attending her "Live Your Best Life Weekend" in New York City. As luck would have it, we ended up in the front row and saw her in person no more than twenty yards away. That had to count as good enough for the life list and I crossed it off, but I felt like a cheat because it wasn't the same as seeing the show.

In May of 2011, Oprah was winding up her long TV run with quite a bit of fanfare. There were special guests on the show all year long and a star-studded tribute to her at the United Center. We tried to get tickets, but failed. Then, four days before the final taping, Lauren called to tell me she had scored Oprah tickets for the final show. I assumed she was a victim of a hoax and did not join in her enthusiasm. The odds of getting a ticket to this once-in- a-lifetime event were like winning the lottery. After trying on a regular basis for a quarter of a century, I found it impossible to believe the hottest tickets in the country landed in her hands. I agreed to accompany her to the studio on the specific date but warned her not to be too disappointed if, when we got there, the doors to the studio were locked. I was sure the final taping had been done the week before and didn't believe this was an actual opportunity.

Of all the life list activities I have completed, I must say this one had the most excitement brewing around it. The slim chance of us achieving this goal, coupled with the fact the final taping was a television milestone, created a once-in-a-lifetime opportunity

Before I knew it the studio doors opened and we were invited in to witness history. Whether you are an Oprah fan or not, one cannot deny the awe of a poor girl from Mississippi navigating a career of influence the way O has done. To watch her skillfully monologue an hour-long program from the heart was like watching a famous artist paint a canvas. It made me feel fortunate to be there. To listen to her craft words into sentences that spoke to each of us differently was like listening to a musician play a concerto, and it made me feel peaceful. But most of all, I experienced an "in the moment" feeling like none I have ever felt before.

We were not allowed to have cell phones or cameras in the studio, so instead of trying to peek through a camera lens, I truly experienced the moment and logged it into memory. The studio only holds about 350 people, so the setting was intimate and every person felt privileged to be there.

We would have experienced none of this if Lauren and I hadn't been working our life lists. The things on my bucket list are how I experience and enjoy life. If I chose not to work my list, I'm afraid one day would blend into the next until the opportunities have passed me by."

Laurie told me that this just wasn't a 'cross off your list' moment, but a game-changer moment for her. It shifted how she saw her life and went for what she wanted – no matter what the odds were against her.

Remember, there are no right or wrong ways to write out your bucket list. No one will judge you. No one will tell you that it's too long or too short. This is only for you. You are only limited by your imagination. In my motivational keynote presentations, I encourage people to be outrageous when setting goals. Don't get caught up being realistic or honest or attainable. You can refine your bucket list of goals later. For now, allow some wild creativity. Go beyond what you think is possible. Allow yourself to dream and dream big. Why not? Go for it!

MY BUCKET LIST

Today's Date: _____

_____

_____

_____

_____

_____

Today's Date: _____

_____

_____

_____

_____

_____

Today's Date: _____

_____

_____

_____

_____

_____

I invite you to come back to your list every year and see your progress. Put a note in your calender to revisit this page. Don't forget to put in your calender where you've stored your book!

For the purpose of this book, I want the focus to be on overcoming the obstacles that have prevented you from attaining your goals. Take a look back over your list. What is the one thing that you've attempted over and over again that you have not been able to accomplish? The one thing that's just out of your reach. As for me, the goal was to reach and maintain my target weight - oh, and speak fluent French. Write down what it is for you.

_____

_____

_____

_____

What do you think is the one thing that has held you back? What has been the one obstacle that if you overcame that, you would be able to accomplish this goal?

_____

_____

In the following chapters, I'm going to discuss how we sabotage our own success. How we each put holes in our own bucket of dreams and allow all our aspirations to leak out. Imagine that each hole is formed by a nail, but we're the ones holding the hammer! As you go through each chapter, I'll start with the self-sabotaging thought or behavior and follow with suggestions on what to do about it. You will find the solution to each situation in each chapter.

Let's get started.

Chapter 2
The SHAME Hole

~

"Shame is the most powerful, master emotion.
It's the fear that we're not good enough."
– Dr. Brené Brown

~

Chapter 2

The SHAME Hole

Shame is a pretty big deal. According to Thomas Scheff, Professor Emeritus of Sociology at UC Santa Barbara, "Shame is the most obstructed and hidden emotion, and therefore the most destructive." In my own case I was ashamed that once again I gained weight and *that* shame contributed to negative self-talk, low energy, and depression; all things that do not serve me as a motivational speaker! Imagine me on stage, sharing messages of hope and inspiration with my audience, telling them that they deserve a front-row seat in life, while still struggling with this one addiction. The shame was overwhelming. I believe it kept me from going for what I really wanted.

When I was researching the effects of shame on human behavior, I found the work of Dr. Brené Brown. She became well known when her TEDX Talk in Houston went viral; with almost seven million views, it's one of the most watched TED talks of all time. You can find it at *https://www.ted.com/playlists/171/the_most_popular_talks_of_all.* Although her talk is called "The Power of Vulnerability," she was really talking about shame. "Shame is the fear of disconnection. It's as if, [if] you knew me, the real me, you may see that I'm not enough. I'm not worthy of that connection that I seek. That fear keeps us from being vulnerable which is necessary for connection," she said.

Shame keeps people from getting the help that they need, because they don't want to admit they need help. Shame loves to keep the secret, and feeds off the self-judgment that comes with the shame. Of course, in my case, it was kind of hard to keep a 32-lb. weight gain a secret. In my industry, it's important to look, feel, and be confident. I'm much more confident when I'm not walking around while suffering the effects of a sugar hangover. My sugar addiction was always indulged in secret, followed by judgment and shame. I'm not alone. Do you remember Luther Vandross? He was an award-winning R&B singer, songwriter, and producer. He had one of the best voices around and his albums never disappointed. I remember going to see him in concert several times, but this one event in San Diego sticks out in my mind. While waiting for the concert to start, I poured through the beautiful picture-filled concert program. There was picture after beautiful picture of Luther at various recent performances. What struck me was how thin he was. He had lost over 100 lbs and he looked fantastic. I had always seen him as being a larger-than-life performer, so it was surprising to see how different he looked. The program included the story of his weight loss and of how proud he was of his healthier lifestyle. Then, he came out on stage. He had gained his weight back. I felt sad for him, because I identified with his struggle. I didn't love him or his music, or his amazing concert, any less. However, I wondered what he must have felt, as he must have known that he no longer looked like his pictures in the program. Did he feel shame? I later found out that he had lost and gained 100lbs - 13 times! I watched an interview in which he said he just didn't like to talk about it, because he knew people could see and might judge him for not being able to beat this one demon. I could relate. When I lost 60 lbs, I got new photos for the covers of my two previous motivational books. After every keynote presentation, I have a book signing where I connect with people one-on-one as I personally sign their books. After gaining half my weight back, I can't help but think that people are judging me because I can't get a handle on this area of my life.

This book is not about weight loss, but that was the catalyst for writing it. That was *my* secret shame. It is hard for me to even write this, because it's so personal. That's the secret power that shame has, though; it loves to attack you in private and convince the little voice in your head that you are not good enough. When you talk about it (or write about it in a book) that little voice is overpowered by evidence to the contrary.

What is *your* secret? What are you afraid you might be judged for, if it was brought to light?

The good news is that we're not alone! Everyone experiences shame. In fact, the only people who don't experience shame are people who are incapable of feeling empathy. Brené Brown says sociopaths are people who don't experience shame. She also affirms the need to shed light on our secrets in her book *Daring Greatly:* "When we bury the story, we forever stay the subject of the story. If we own the story, we get to narrate the ending."

My friend and colleague Kirsty Spraggon can attest to this as well. She was a very successful businesswoman in real estate and started her own TV Show, called *Kirsty TV.* She interviewed people - get this- on the power of sharing secrets. She had a huge following but hid her own secret. She allowed the shame of that secret to rule her life for 18 years. It wasn't until she took the leap and told people about her secret that she was able to live on the other side of the fear. You certainly don't have go on TV to share your secret, but use Kirsty as an example. Once her secret was revealed, she no longer had to numb her pain, but enjoyed the freedom that authenticity brought her. Kirsty's story reminds us that when we numb the pain of our shame, we also numb the joy of our life.

Patching the hole created by shame:

Shame lives in secret and in the dark and is fed by judgment. Here are my solutions to the obstacle of shame:

1. Shed light on the shame by talking about it. Share your secret with someone you trust. You just may be able to connect with someone on a deeper, less superficial level. You don't have to do a YouTube video, or post it on Facebook. You can just disclose your feelings of shame to someone that you know will have empathy for you. Someone who will sit with you, be present with you and say, "I hear you. I feel you." Maybe you'll hear them say, "I've been there, too." When you shed light on your shame, its power goes away. Don't hang on to the safety of it, let it go. You will find that when you talk about it to a non-judgmental friend, counselor, or trusted spiritual advisor, the power it had over you immediately dissipates.

   Be careful, though, in whom you confide. I had a friend tell me that you don't go to a dry well for water! That makes sense. You can't go to someone for unconditional love and support, or joy and celebration, if they are judgmental, hurtful, unsympathetic people with the sensitivity of a gnat. Unfortunately, sometimes we are related to these people. If so, we need to love them from a distance by setting some boundaries. Make sure you are equipped with a solid foundation of support if you have to be around them at a wedding, or a funeral, for example. You don't need anyone triggering your shame by adding guilt, resulting in more shame that will make you retreat back into the shame hole.

2. Seek out others who have experienced what you have. You will quickly see that you are not alone. Every successful person I know who has crossed things off their bucket list has stories of their struggle. Everyone has had to overcome something to get to where they are today. Seek them out. Study them. Learn from them. If they are available, reach out to them.

3. Ask for help. It's a lot easier to be the helper than the helpee. It takes courage and strength to admit that you need help, but when you risk the vulnerability to ask for help, it gives you strength. There is strength and power that comes from overcoming your fear and getting to the answer; then, there is power in the answer! When you know more, you do more. Seek out those answers by asking for help.

4. Know that you are good enough. Taking some sort of action is better than no action. My friend, Jessica Pettitt, wrote a book called *Good Enough Now*. "Once shame is tamed," she said, "we must lean into it and begin to try. The keeping up of trying becomes the goal instead of perfection or failure." I like that, because a lot of people feel that they need to be perfect to be good enough, when in fact they - and you - are good enough now. Or, they feel that if people knew their shame, people wouldn't consider them good enough to get what they want.

5. Practice compassion. When we're feeling shame we take the judgment that we learned early - the same judgment that caused the shame in the first place - and pile it on to where we not only think ourselves unworthy of success, but wonder *who do we think we are to even* **want** *it?* Be gentle on yourself; show compassion when those self-limiting beliefs come to mind.

Social psychologist, Kristin Neff, discovered that self-compassion can act as an antidote to the self-criticism that comes with shame. When you start thinking of all your failures and how that means you are a bad person, stop and remind yourself of how far you've come, how much work you have done. Celebrate your small successes. Celebrate the 'try' in you and the optimism that you'll never give up.

6. Focus on your goodness. The name of my first company was called, "Stay Focused Seminars" because I believed you got what you focused on. When you look for negative, you'll find it. When you look for positive, you'll find that too. The next time you feel criticized by someone, remind yourself of your many other talents. For example, when someone critiques or makes a joke about my cooking skills - or lack thereof - I am pretty good with a comeback. "I have a lot of talents, but cooking just isn't one of them." I acknowledge that I don't cook well, but I have no desire to learn! (It's certainly not on my bucket list.) My point being, I don't attach judgment to it and then think I'm a bad person.

We can do the same with the one thing we're ashamed of, if we are struggling with something that is tripping us up. It would be easy to lump it in with other inadequacies; in fact, I call that 'horriblizing' an event or a situation. (I know it's not a word, but I can't think of a word that describes taking one problem and adding problems on top of it and others on top of that.) You don't need to heap every single one of your shortcomings onto one ultimate shame pile; that would make it difficult for anyone to crawl out from underneath. Separate out one thing that you know you need to work on. Get some help around that. Admit your struggle with the hope that you want to get better and decide you want to change for the better. If those negative thoughts of shame come up, recognize them as something belonging to the past. Acknowledge that you are working on it and you're a better person today than you were yesterday. Remind yourself that you have decided to make better choices from here on out.

Patch the hole in your bucket list that was created by shame. Patch it with love and kindness and grace. Forgive yourself for your past, while recognizing that you are a different person today. Today, you are strong. Today, you can look forward in confidence, because you no longer have shame taking power away from you. That hole that allowed your dreams to leak out of your bucket has been patched up with compassion and joy.

Here's where the healing begins.

Chapter 2 Wrap-Up:

1. Shed light by talking about your secret shame
2. Seek out others with similar secrets
3. Ask for help
4. Know that you're good enough
5. Practice compassion
6. Focus on your goodness

Chapter 3
The COMPARISON Hole

~

"No one has the right to burst your bubble of enthusiasm."
– Marilyn de Boisredon

~

Chapter 3
The COMPARISON Hole

Here's the thing about comparison: when you compare yourself to other people, you never come out equal. You always come out either better than, or less than, and neither one is healthy. What does that have to do with your bucket list of dreams? Sometimes, when we have our goals and wishes for what we want to accomplish in our life, it takes courage to put ourselves out there to make them happen. We take risks. We work toward something. We ask for the sale, or for the job; we promote our idea. When we put ourselves out there we're vulnerable to rejection. This, in turn, feeds our insecurities. It's human nature that we see others out there, doing what *we* want to do and compare ourselves to them. We get competitive, jealous, envious, and that allows doubt and fear to seep in. None of which serves us.

When we compare ourselves to others, we can only compare what we see of them and what we know of ourselves. If we think they are better than us, we get insecure and intimidated by their success. If we are intimidated by their success, we aren't going to approach them and ask for help, for a referral, for coaching or for 5 minutes to run an idea by them over a cup of coffee. We then sabotage ourselves for no other reason than because we made up a false comparison.

Then we make assumptions. For example, "If I'm here at this level and they're at that level, they aren't going to want to help me." Again, comparing leads to inactivity - which sounds like an oxymoron.

Back in the day, comparisons would be about who had the better car, house, boyfriend, girlfriend, spouse, body, bank account, etc. Today? The comparison could be all of those things, plus seeing how we live our life compared to how others lead theirs, as shown daily on social media! There is status attached to how many followers you have on Instagram, Twitter, and your YouTube channel. Then, there is the phenomenon of Facebook. Not only are we comparing how many likes, shares, and updates people have, but also the extravagant, sometimes exaggerated, and often embellished lifestyle that people are posting about. All of this anxiety causes distress. In fact, "Facebook Envy," is now a thing. You see people you know, who are posting photos of their new car, their new home, their new shopping spree; maybe having an amazing vacation, sipping champagne in a first class cabin. People get envious of the lifestyle they see posted *every single day* and they get sad because their life isn't like that. Our society is becoming more obsessed with lifestyles that aren't normal. Have you seen an episode of Keeping Up With The Kardashians? Take a glance at any of the Real Housewives reality series. They are a look into the lives of people in their own habitat that everyday average people cannot relate to in any way. When you watch these shows, you can't help but compare your own home to theirs, your own car to theirs, etc. Even when the Kardashian sisters are having a casual conversation out on the patio with the kids running around, you see how pretty they are and that their hair and makeup are flawless. What you *don't* see is that there is a whole team of people who are employed to do their hair and make-up. They have their glam-squads with them every day. They don't even have normal bathrooms in their homes, they have salon-quality glam rooms with professional-grade lights, makeup, and hair stations. The point to remember is that when you see a post, a selfie, or a snap of someone's life, that's just what it is: a snapshot. Don't read into it to the extent that you compare yourself to them and, by extension, your life to theirs. What you don't know is what happened right before that photo was taken. You don't know the full story. You don't need to compare, thinking "Wow, why don't *I* look like that?" You probably *could* look like that if you had a team of people professionally making you up every day.

Facebook was originally created for connection. Use it for that purpose; to connect, stay connected, re-connect, inspire or be inspired. If you find yourself feeling sad or depressed, chances are you're falling into the comparison trap. In order to work your way out of it, monitor how much time you spend on social media. Maybe lurking has turned into your obsession and hours go by, whereas you could have used that time more constructively. Actually, the same could be said for watching reality TV. Yes, I know people watch it for an escape from their own reality, but when you start to compare your life to what you see and it makes you sad, then it's time for a reality check - and a reality TV diet. If you need to have your fix, checking in on social media or catching up on TV, maybe you could counter that with equal time dedicated to doing something positive. Reading positive, mind-stretching materials, or watching something that expands your learning. Maybe you could even set the same amount of time working toward crossing something off your bucket list.

As I mentioned in the previous chapter about Jess Pettitt's book *Good Enough Now*, if we feel positive and confident about who we are right *now,* than we don't need to expend any energy comparing ourselves to others. It's okay that we don't drive the newest car, or possess the latest designer pick of the week. There is freedom when we let go of the need to keep up with other people. So when you do see a post about a friend's fancy car, or hear about a huge contract a competitor signed, don't internalize it at all. Separate how you feel for them - happy for them, proud of them, in awe of them - and how you feel about yourself, (*I'm on my own path, on my own journey, and will arrive in my own time.*)

I know someone who has lots and lots of clothes. She has so many clothes that they don't fit in her home, so she had to rent a couple of storage units to store all of them. I lost count of just her black slacks! I couldn't believe how many pairs of black pants she had. I didn't realize people needed that many things to wear. When I made the comment "You have more clothes than anyone I've ever met in my life," her response surprised me. She said, "Well, I don't have as many as my neighbor. You should see her closet!" I couldn't believe that she was comparing how many clothes she had to how many clothes her neighbor had. It was as if there was a competition with prizes handed out for all to see.

I, too, have friends with amazing closets, but I don't look at theirs and compare them to mine and make a judgment. It doesn't make sense. It is an excuse to make yourself feel bad when you don't have what you want. Then you compile evidence of what others have that you don't. It's a no-win situation that, again, doesn't serve you.

One of the downsides of comparison is envy. When we envy someone else's success, for example, it causes us distress. This increases our resentment of them, which increases the potential for feeling anger toward them. When we're envious, we tend to distance ourselves from that person because we don't want them to know we're envious of their work, recognition, or success. Of course, this will now undermine our own success. When we focus too intently on others, we are no longer focusing on what *we* need to do to succeed, especially if we feel threatened by their success. To reiterate, comparison can lead to envy, which can lead to resentment, which in turn leads to anger. If we continue, we might then add guilt and shame to the mix, which will ultimately bring our self-respect down. Wow. No wonder envy is known as one of the seven deadly sins.

How do you know if you are secretly envious of someone else? Look at someone who is attempting to do what you secretly want to do. If their attempt fails, do you quietly celebrate? There's a red flag! If they succeed, do you feel bad that it wasn't you? Do you feel sad and a little depressed? There's a sign! Do you talk about them behind their back, offering unkind explanations for their success or failure? If you are envious of someone and you distance yourself from them, then there is no way you would approach them for feedback, help, mentorship, or coaching. That would surely be a missed opportunity. As you can see, being envious or jealous does not serve you, it doesn't move you forward toward accomplishing your own dreams or goals. On the other hand, if you are confident within yourself, if you are secure with your own journey, independent of other people's, then when *they* succeed you can be truly happy for them. When they fail, you can feel sincere compassion for them.

Celebrate others successes, not their failures.

Patching the hole created by Comparison:

Here's how to patch the comparison hole in your bucket list. Look at your bucket list. Pick something on your list that you want to cross off, then go find someone who HAS accomplished it. Read up on them, study them, and find out about their journey. What did they have to do? What did they have to overcome? How did they tackle adversity? Maybe it's a person in history - read biographies on them. Maybe it's an author - read his or her autobiography. Maybe it's a colleague that you've admired from a distance because they are farther ahead in their career than you are in yours. Connect with them on LinkedIn. Call them up, and ask them how they did it! Get out of your comfort zone, accept that you are on a journey with no judgment and seek out the support of others that are farther along their journey than you. Ask for help. Go for it.

The key to letting go of comparison and envy of others is knowing that there will always be someone smarter than you. There will always be someone richer than you. There will always be someone who has more than you. However, the same that could be said for people looking at YOU. There are probably people who look at you, your lifestyle, your home, and think that YOU have it all! You are the ideal! When I was walking around calling myself a walking "before" picture, I could have been someone else's goal. No matter what we complain that we don't have, it's probably a first-world problem. If you are complaining about not getting that upgrade on a flight, or not getting recognized at an event, or someone getting a larger bonus than you, imagine someone in a third-world country uttering those same exact words. It really puts your life into perspective.

My parents actually taught me that lesson when I was 16 years old.

It was so powerful; I remember it to this day. My parents valued a U.S education and they wanted my siblings and I to take it seriously. To reinforce that, they took us on a trip outside of the United States. Specifically, they wanted us to learn about other cultures. We grew up in a community called Mercer Island, near Seattle. It's known as an affluent area. Some outsiders jokingly called it "Poverty Rock." My parents didn't want to raise spoiled children and thought exposure to other cultures - ones that didn't have it so good - would shift our perspective and help us appreciate what we had here. Hopefully, we would then be more inclined to take advantage of the educational opportunities our country had to offer. We kids were taken on these trips in turns, usually right before our senior year in high school. My mother and father were already in the travel business and this made it easier for us. Dad was in the air-freight industry. Mom owned her own travel company and took private tours to Asia and Europe. When it was my turn, I was fortunate enough to have my mom to take me on a private tour of her favorite places in the Far East. Looking back on it now, this itinerary must surely be on someone's bucket list today. We started in Taipei, Taiwan. Next, off to Seoul, South Korea, then Hong Kong, with our final destination being Tokyo and Kyoto, Japan. It really was a cultural awakening for me. My parents were right. I had lived a pretty sheltered life and this was before access to YouTube, where today you can see with a few clicks how people live in places all over the world.

When we went into the mountains of South Korea, I saw villages where the sewer system was the street. I had never before seen families sleeping on floors made of mud. My eyes were opened to a world beyond what I was used to and I was inspired. I was grateful for the life I had at home, and grateful for the roof over our head. In addition my eyes were opened in another way. When I saw the crowds of Tokyo, motorbikes in Taiwan, and the beauty to be seen taking the Star Ferry to Hong Kong Island, my eyes were opened to the possibilities of what was out there in the world. My parents worked very hard in the travel and air-freight industries so they saw a lot of the world. This trip taught me that if I too, worked hard, more opportunity would be available to me as well. Can you be sad when you see someone who has what you want? Sure, but don't dwell on it. Turn it around and look at what you have to be grateful for. What do you feel fortunate to have? Break it down to the essentials if you have to. The next time you want to compare yourself to someone else, choose to let his or her life be an example of what is possible. Choose to be grateful for the opportunity that you have in front of you. I've never forgotten that. No matter what I'm going through, I know that I have a roof over my head, food on the table, and fresh drinking water available to me. No matter what, someone in the world has it worse than me, just because of where they were born. Therefore, I'm blessed and lucky, so I'm not going to waste a single second of the opportunity I have on this earth in comparing myself to another person.

What about if others compare you to other people?

There is only so much you can do when other people compare you to others. *Why can't you be like your brother? Why can't you be like your sister?* How about when you start to evolve and grow and other people don't like it: *Why can't you be like before?*

These are really loaded questions. One answer is to simply say - without getting too defensive or emotional - "I'm doing the best that I can." Remember it's called a comparison trap for a reason! It's a trap; so don't get caught in it. After all, how does it feel when we get trapped? We panic and it doesn't feel good. The next time someone tries to compare you to someone else, just love on them and ask yourself later if you have to be near them. The older I get, the more I realize I don't have to be around people who demean me or put me down or judge me in a negative way. I can love them from a distance, plant them firmly in the balcony, and not let them into the front-row of my life - if you know what I mean. That's prime real estate and should be reserved for the people in your life who love you unconditionally. Keep that space reserved for people who make you feel good about who you are. When comparison gets you down, count your blessings and put your life into perspective.

Chapter 3 Wrap-Up:

1. See yourself as an incomparable individual
2. Seek out successful people and learn from them
3. Celebrate the successes of others, instead of being envious - don't distance yourself from them
4. Ask for help from others who have what you want
5. Accept where you are today, knowing it's better than yesterday and not as good as tomorrow
6. Stop comparing yourself to others
7. Know that your journey is your journey
8. Others are on their own journey
9. No one has the right to judge your journey, no need for you to either
10. Go on a social-media diet
11. Fill your brain with learning

Chapter 4
The NEGATIVITY Hole

~

"One cannot be prepared for something while
secretly believing it will not happen."
– Nelson Mandela

~

Chapter 4

The NEGATIVITY Hole

I asked an audience recently if they had a bucket list. One guy in my audience asked, "Written down?" A woman said she had one, but it hadn't been updated in years. A third person said, "I never wrote down my bucket list, because that would make it real. My fear of commitment keeps me from writing anything down." Finally, another person said, "My fear kept my bucket list in my drawer. Deep down, I didn't think I could accomplish what was on it."

When you are positive, you will create more opportunities for yourself. I remember one time I was flying to Seattle, and for some reason, I booked my ticket far too late in the day for the meeting I was attending. Luckily, it wasn't a speaking engagement. However, it would still have been inconvenient if I were late. I went to the airport really early, to go on standby for the earlier flight. I went to the ticket counter and was put on the standby list and was told to go wait at the gate. The agent did warn me that there were already 15 people ahead of me so it didn't look likely that I would make it on that flight, but maybe I would make the next one. I was positive and optimistic because, in all circumstances, it doesn't help to be negative! I sat at the gate, watching them board the 7:00 am flight. They boarded and boarded and boarded and I saw the waiting list for standby passengers. There were so many people waiting, with so few seats available! They called one name from the standby list, then another. Then, they did it; they closed the door to the jet way. That is never a good sign. The announcement soon followed. "All standby passengers, this flight to Seattle has checked in full. Please proceed to the other terminal for the next flight to Seattle at 10:00." I didn't move. First off, I was shocked I hadn't made the flight. I had been positive I was going to make the flight. I had hoped and hoped that I would make that flight, and I still had a positive feeling that I *would* make that flight, so I just sat there, even after they shut that door to the jet way.

Then, it happened.

The door opened!

A flight attendant came off the flight with a passenger, literally escorting her off the plane. I went to the gate agent and said "Can I have her seat?" The gate agent asked my name and saw that I was still 10 people down on the list and told me so. I looked around the boarding area and there wasn't a soul left. She looked at me and said "It's your lucky day!" I boarded the flight, ecstatic that I was going to be in Seattle on time. Then, when I took that newly vacated seat, I had to ask the people next to me "What happened to the woman who was sitting here?" They told me she was escorted off the plane for public intoxication. Wow! I didn't see that one coming.

I know this example is sort of out of the ordinary, but is it? When you start with the positive expectancy of your desired outcome, you act different. You interact with others different. I know people who claim that they always get a parking spot right where and when they need one. There is something to be said for having a positive expectancy: you expect something good to happen like a job to be offered to you, a relationship to work, or a parking spot to open up.

If your outcome is influenced in any way by another person, being positive is an absolute necessity, especially when it comes to travel. People are so rude and impatient in airports, hotels, and restaurants. I've witnessed this over the 20-plus years of traveling for speaking engagements. I've had people thank me for my patience or upgrade me because of my attitude during a trying time. You really can get so much further with people when you show a positive attitude, even in the face of frustration. Have a positive expectation that you can, in fact, have your bucket list of dreams come true. You can experience your dreams and heart's desires. You can go for it. It must start with a positive mindset. Norman Vincent Peale, as you probably know, was the founder of the self-help genre and wrote a book called, *The Power of Positive Thinking*. Although his work was originally published in 1952, it still holds up today. For example, here's a gem from his book:

"Formulate and stamp indelibly on your mind a mental picture of yourself as succeeding. Hold this picture tenaciously. Never permit it to fade. Your mind will seek to develop the picture...do not build up obstacles in your imagination."

Here's another:

"When you expect the best, you release a magnetic force in your mind which by a law of attraction tends to bring the best to you."

Yes, this was written many years before the law of attraction became more of a mainstream conversation.

What does this mean for you?

Make sure that you have a positive foundation in your belief system. That what you want to create for your life and the life of your family, community, work, (whatever is touched by the success of you living and succeeding with your bucket list) is possible. Not only is it possible, but it is possible for you. When you start with a positive mindset, it changes not only how you approach your list, but perhaps what's on your list. It would be interesting to see how your list changes after you read this book. If you were to write your list with the mindset that whatever you wrote, you would succeed, what would THAT list look like?

Once you have that belief that success is indeed possible, then you will talk differently about your list. Instead of saying "One day…" you might put a timeline on it. "By this time next year…." Instead of saying "I hope to…," you would say "I will."

The next time negative thoughts try to punch holes in your bucket of dreams, just stop them. Jack Canfield, an author and professional speaker, suggests that you actually say, "Cancel. Cancel." When you allow a negative thought to come to your mind, or out of your mouth, shift your mindset quickly. Don't get in the habit of negative self-talk. Thoughts become beliefs and beliefs determine your actions. Keep your thoughts positive, so you can keep moving toward accomplishing those things on your bucket list.

When you wake up every day in a positive frame of mind you will be more likely to follow a positive plan that will move you closer to your goal, because you know in your heart that you will achieve it. When you believe in yourself, thinking and talking more positively, you behave differently. You walk into rooms differently. You walk into sales presentations differently. There's more of an aura of confidence surrounding you, more of a shine of positive expectancy that radiates from you. Then, hopefully, you'll notice that your language will shift. You will go from, "Oh, things like that never happen to me." to "Yes! I'm going to go for that contract!" Or from, "I'll never be able to reach that." to "I plan on hitting that benchmark next quarter." When you walk different and talk different, something happens, something about which I need to warn you.

Other people.

This is where it gets tricky. You're ready to set your bucket list in motion. You've got it written out. You've pictured what success looks like, you've visualized even that ONE thing that has eluded you, and you are going for it. You are going to tackle it and share your newfound confidence and positive mindset with other people. They react. Maybe they're supportive. Maybe not.

Maybe they say:

- No way - not you
- You're too old
- You're too young
- You're too fat
- You're too thin
- You're too broke
- You're too busy
- You're too uneducated
- That's too unrealistic
- Really? Again? Didn't you already try that?
- No one's done that before

The list goes on and on. Sometimes, out of jealousy, people will push your buttons with comments, insults, jabs, or anything to get you off your game. Sometimes it's so subtle you don't even realize how their lack of support is eroding your confidence. Then you start to second-guess what's possible.

My particular favorite is, "Who do you think you are?" That one cuts deep. The person that says that to you doesn't even need to finish the sentence. If you're vulnerable to - or vested in their opinion of you, then you can probably finish the sentence yourself. *"Maybe they're right. Who am I, to think that I can accomplish this? Who am I, to even think that I can try? Who do I think I am anyway?"* Nothing good comes from that internal dialogue. There's no winning that conversation. Furthermore, because of their jealousy, they will want to see you fail, so they can feel better about themselves. Sometimes people sabotage you just so they can say, "See, I told you so." How they feel about themself is not your responsibility. No one, no matter what his or her intention or motive is, has the right to burst your bubble of enthusiasm.

Sometimes, people will take a shot at your dreams trying to discourage you, out of anger. Take my friend and colleague, Jason Hewlett. He was succeeding as an entertainer for the show, "Legends in Concert," impersonating Ricky Martin and Elton John. He is very talented and wanted to expand his offering and do more of a variety show, impersonating lots of great talents. He honed his skills, travelling around the country performing for any audience that would watch. Then he got his big break. He was offered a decade-long contract, a headlining act in Las Vegas. This was his dream! He would be the next Danny Gans, and he would be set for life. Unfortunately, the contract wouldn't allow him to have creative control of the content, whereas he insisted on having a clean show.

He knew he wanted his kids to one day see his show and always be proud of their dad, and he vowed he would always be family-friendly on stage. The producer said he wasn't famous enough to make such demands and he had to sign the contract "as is."

Jason Hewlett stood by his convictions and didn't sign the contract.

The producer of the show was obviously upset and told Jason he would never headline in Vegas, ever.

Fast-forward to a dozen years later. Jason continued to work on his act, perfecting his impersonations, adding some motivation to his message, and is now one of the best corporate entertainer/ speakers I've ever seen in my life. The man is so talented, and so funny, that

I'm in awe every time I see him perform. He now has clients all over the world, in addition to headlining corporate events in, yes, Las Vegas. It was a special joy for me to see him inducted to the National Speakers Association Speaker Hall of Fame. What a journey to witness. I can't even imagine what the world would have lost if Jason would have listened to the man that threatened him with, "You'll never work in this town again."

Sometimes people are not supportive of your dreams because they've simply never seen them before. Maybe what you're proposing simply takes someone out of his or her comfort zone and they don't know how to support you in your efforts. For example: Criquette and Treve. It's an amazing story about a girl and a horse. (By the way, Criquette is the girl.) Christiane "Criquette" Head grew up in the countryside of France, coming from a family of horse breeders, trainers, and jockeys. When her father retired from competitive horse racing, he bred and trained racehorses. She loved watching and learning from him. He taught her how to see what was special in each horse and how each horse needed to be handled differently. One day she declared to her father that she, too, wanted to grow up and train horses just like him. In those days, there were no women horse trainers. He suggested that, if she wanted to be in the horse-training industry, she should grow up and marry a horse trainer, but that's not what she wanted. She convinced her dad that she was serious about taking on the industry herself. He then supported her by teaching her everything he knew. She started to show promise by watching and noticing differences in the horses they were training. Like anyone with a passion for what they do, she dedicated her time and energy to learning everything about the industry. She worked as an assistant trainer for her dad at first, but wanted to be licensed herself. She filled out all the paperwork and applied for her credentials. Much to her surprise, she was denied certification as a horse trainer. She confronted the committee and asked why she was denied the license. Wasn't everything in order? Yes, everything was in order. The only thing that kept her from being approved was the fact that she was a woman. They had never ever, granted a business license to a woman to train horses.

Criquette wouldn't take no for an answer. She made a deal with them. She suggested, since everyone had to renew their licenses every year anyway, that they grant her a license for a year and then, if she didn't produce, they didn't have to renew her license. They agreed. The following year, a horse Criquette trained - owned by her mother and ridden by her brother - won the most prestigious horse race in France, the Prix de l'Arc de Triomphe. She had no problem renewing her license after that. Nonetheless, it wasn't always easy for Criquette.

In 2011, Criquette brought one of her horses to the Arqana yearling sale in Deauville, France, to auction. Treve was a three-year-old bay who was sired by Motivator. Now you know why I was drawn to this story! I don't know why, but no one bid on Treve. No one. I don't know if they thought a filly bred and trained by Criquette was less valuable than the other horses up for auction that day, but no one bid on her. Criquette bought Treve back from auction for the minimum bid of €22,000 Euros (approximately $26,000 U.S.). For comparison, another horse named Chiquita sold at that same auction house 2 months earlier for €600,000 Euros (Approximately $709,000 U.S.). Criquette continued to train Treve and they started to win. And, win again. And again. Treve won a prestigious European race called the Prix de Diane. Who took 2nd place that day? Chiquita. Treve went on to win the Prix de l'Arc de Triomphe, solidifying Criquette's reputation as one of the best trainers around. Treve was sold for a significant amount of money, but the new owners wanted Criquette to continue to train Treve. In the following year (2014) Treve won the Prix de l'Arc de Triomphe for the second year in a row! That hadn't happened in over 38 years. Treve was named Cartier Horse of the Year and Criquette was named Trainer of the Year. This little horse that no one bid on at $26,000 earned over $7,093,000 for her owners. I had the pleasure of meeting Criquette at her horse farm in Chantille, France, where she introduced me to Motivator and Treve. While she was telling me the story of this incredible horse - who, by the way, was putting on a show for us in the pasture with her stable mate - I casually made the obvious comment, "I bet the people who were at that auction house in 2011 wish they had bid on Treve at the time." She laughed and said, "They don't admit they were there!"

I love this story for so many reasons - and not just because it's about horses.

It's about:

1. Perseverance
2. Succeeding against all odds
3. Being an underdog and going for it anyway
4. Winning when people are against you
5. Investing in your dreams
6. Not taking no for an answer
7. Following your passion
8. Convincing others that you know what you're doing and to trust you with their asset

Patching the hole of negativity:

It all starts with you. Start making sure *now* that the thoughts you allow into your mind are positive, productive, supportive, nurturing, constructive, helpful, graceful, and loving. Affirm your uniqueness in the world and how you deserve the best life has to offer. Every day, wake up with the determination to make the best of every circumstance and don't waste a minute allowing your focus to go to the dark side.

What should you do the next time other people start with their negative comments? Assess where they are coming from. Let them know you don't agree with them, or that you don't appreciate the negativity. You might ask them if they're okay. Sometimes, out of their own pain, people lash out at people like you. If that's the case, maybe they need some help; an encouraging word, a kind gesture, or even a silent prayer.

One thing that will help you stay positive on a daily basis, even in the face of other people who aren't so positive, is to keep a "win-list." I've talked about this for years and even wrote about it in my first book, *Whose Comfort Zone Are You In?* Every night, just jot down the things that went right in your day. During the day, if you have an amazing thing happen, grab your "win-list" and add to it. If something unexpected happened that made your day, write that down. If someone gives you a nice compliment or shows you some unexpected kindness, write that down. Pretty soon, you'll not only have a journal of positive thoughts and expressions, or examples of love and support, but your brain will be conditioned to see goodness around you. Again, you get what you focus on; the more you focus on the positive, the more positive you will see. The extra benefit to having this "win-list" handy is that it will act as an protective armor when someone shocks you with a discouraging remark, an insult, or slam against your dreams. You won't be as quick to buy into the negativity because you'll have all this evidence that you've collected. Try it. It really, really works. I'm positive.

Chapter 4 Wrap-Up:

1. Shift your mindset to focus on the positive
2. Shift your language to be more positive
3. Stand by your convictions
4. Believe that your goals can become your reality
5. Wake up every day and affirm the positive
6. Keep a win-list of all the things that are going right in your day
7. Review your win-list frequently

Chapter 5
The FEAR hole

~

*"Courage is resistance to fear, mastery
of fear, not absence of fear."*
– Mark Twain

~

~

*"Start by doing what's necessary; then do what's
possible; and suddenly you are doing the impossible."*
– Saint Francis of Assisi

~

Chapter 5

The FEAR hole

When I speak at conferences about getting a front-row seat in life, I explain that a front-row seat is where you get to say, "It doesn't get any better than this." When I ask my audiences what prevents people from getting that front-row seat they desire, the number one answer is ALWAYS fear.

No hesitation. Fear. What are people so afraid of?

Most commonly, people are afraid of failure. How would it make them look to try something and fail at it? No one likes to be seen as a failure and many people still attach their self-worth to success, instead of seeing themselves as courageous for trying. If you look, for example, at any successful leader and ask them if they've ever failed, I guarantee you they will say not only, "Yes," but also "frequently." You see, we cannot learn, or grow, or even build character from sitting on the sideline.

I asked some people what prevented them from reaching their goals. One response I found particularly saddening. One woman told me "Fear, lack of self-confidence, and sometimes, I know what I should do to accomplish that goal, but I don't because, sometimes, not trying at all is better than failing." I disagree wholeheartedly. The opposite of lack of self-confidence is competence. If you know how to do something well, you're confident you can do it. You probably have little fear of failure, because of your confidence that you are competent. Therefore, the answer is to do what you know how to do, then add to what you know a little at a time, to increase your competence. The more you increase your competence the more you increase your confidence.

When it comes to fear, I think people assume that successful people don't ever feel it, because things seem to come to them naturally and easily. People think, "Oh, look how lucky they are!" NO! They *do* have fear, but they face the fear, knowing that there is excitement and achievement right on the other side.

We grow and build by trying, creating, failing, learning; then by trying, creating, failing, learning; over and over again; and by celebrating the little successes along the way.

What's wrong with staying safe? What's wrong with not trying at all? What's wrong is that you get left behind. Once, I asked a mixed corporate audience what percentage of readiness did they have to have before they would take on a stretch job or a promotion. The answers from the men were pretty low - around 40-80%. One guy stopped me in my tracks when he said 0%. I asked him to clarify. It turned out that, before he took his corporate job, he played in the highly competitive world of professional sports. He was successful at it, too. His attitude was, "I know I have the potential to learn and excel in any job, given the chance." His answer wasn't common, but I loved it. He had no fear of taking on stretch jobs knowing he could learn and adapt.

Then, I asked the ladies to chime in, and they collectively said 100%. Now, this was not a scientific study, it was an observation of men and women working in different organizations who were at a professional development training day. If we were to dig deeper, we would see that sometimes men overestimate their qualifications and think they can throw their hat in the ring on a job opportunity, based only on their potential. They may see the required qualifications listed on the application as being flexible, anticipating they will show their potential in the interview. Women sometimes are more likely to follow the rules and to assume the qualifications listed are actually required; they might not want to waste the interviewer's time, or their own time, by applying and being denied. Fear of breaking rules, of being denied, all contribute to people from not taking risks and getting what they want out of their careers.

I saw an executive on a panel at a women's conference who told the story of a posh position with a corner office that came open in her company. She knew a woman that she thought would be perfect for that job. Before the job was posted a man came to her and asked to be considered for it. She later went to the woman she'd had in mind for the position and asked the woman why she hadn't ever approached management to at least discuss the open position (where it sounded like it was hers for the taking). She said she wasn't ready, didn't think she was qualified.

If any of us, men or women, wait until we know how to do something perfectly before we try it, we'll never try it. We have to get out of our comfort zone. You know, that place where everything is familiar. My mentor, Dr. Nido Qubein says that your comfort zone leads to habits and habits lead to mediocrity. Who wants to live anywhere near mediocrity? It's time to stretch outside of that comfort zone. In fact, that's where people say success lies - right outside of your comfort zone.

If you were to look at anyone's bucket list, I doubt that anything listed would be considered inside of their comfort zone. Remember the examples of what people put on their bucket lists from earlier? I doubt any of these are in the comfort zone of the people who wrote them down:

1. Skydiving
2. Hot air balloon over the Serengeti during the Great Migration
3. Dive the Great Barrier Reef
4. Pilgrimage of Santiago de Compostela
5. Speak to an audience of 30,000 people
6. Walk on the Great Wall of China
7. Visiting gorillas in their habitat
8. Land and takeoff from an aircraft carrier in a fighter jet
9. Ride an elephant in the jungle
10. Storm chasing
11. Try out for a play
12. Complete an ironman competition
13. Run in the Boston Marathon
14. Live in Yosemite National Park for a full year
15. Take $100 and travel the world for a year

∼

"Character cannot be developed in ease and quiet. Only through experience of trial and suffering can the soul be strengthened, ambition inspired, and success achieved."
– Helen Keller

∼

By the way, not everyone is afraid of failure. There are people who are paralyzed by fear of success. They know what it's like to fail, they can deal with the known. What they don't know is, what if they succeed at something? That is unchartered territory. That fear of the unknown can be immobilizing to some. Plus, if they do succeed, there may be pressure to continue to succeed and they don't know if they could handle that pressure. What if it's too much? Fear ends up being the reason why people stay in:

- The same roles
- The same jobs
- The same relationships
- The same partnerships
- At same companies
- The same cities
- The same routines

Even though they may not be entirely satisfied, they stick around because clinging to what they know is easier than facing the fear of what they don't know.

What's wrong with staying in a place where you're not happy or satisfied, despite knowing there is something better for you out there? I think, little by little, it kills your spirit and joy. Your enthusiasm for that role or job or relationship wanes and eventually fails. That lack of forward momentum will stall your movement toward joy, and will work against you in other areas of your life.

Let's say that, in order to fulfill one of your dreams, you have to confront someone and have a really difficult conversation. The fear of rejection or hurt or disappointment is so strong that you would rather avoid the conversation, put your dreams away in a drawer, and live your life as is. The problem with that is that repressed anger and resentment and frustration will build up and come to the surface. Maybe you'll see others living in their joy, doing what they want with their life and feeling happy and free - as you would like to be doing - and so feelings of jealousy and envy creep in. All of these emotions do not serve you and only make your situation worse, and for what? To avoid the possibility of a briefly uncomfortable conversation? I guess the purpose of what I'm saying here is to get you to ask yourself how much more of your life are you willing to spend in a place that is not satisfying or rewarding? When you look at your options - staying where you are vs. taking a risk and moving through the fear - what are the consequences over the long term? Imagine you have a fear that's keeping you from doing something that you know you want and need to do. You decide to do nothing. Now fast-forward five years from today. How would your life be, if you hadn't acted on your fear? How about 10 years? Thinking of the conversation you need to have, or the confrontation you need to face, and it makes you cringe, right? However, if avoiding that conflict keeps you trapped in a situation that will ultimately rob you of your joy, then you are not honoring yourself. If you have children, think of the message you're sending by staying in your fear. If you don't have children, think of your own destiny; is this the life you want to live? Does worrying about what others think influence your decisions as to how you live your life? If so, consider what Apple Co-founder Steve Jobs said during his 2005 Stanford Commencement speech.

"Remembering that I'll be dead soon is the most important tool I've ever encountered to help me make the big choices in life. Because almost everything - all external expectations, all pride, all fear of embarrassment or failure - these things just fall away in the face of death, leaving only what is truly important. Your time is limited, so don't waste it living someone else's life. Don't let the noise of others' opinions drown out your own inner voice. And most important, have the courage to follow your heart and intuition. They somehow already know what you truly want to become. Everything else is secondary."

I don't mean to sound morbid, and certainly the very definition of a bucket list is, "things to do before death," but you don't have to wait for a death sentence. You don't have to wait for a near-death experience to see the wisdom of making important choices in order to live your life exactly how you want, based on *your* values and what is important to *you*. In fact, that's another good reason to have a bucket list; to remind yourself what's really important in your life. This is why you are working so hard, so you can enjoy amazing adventures with your family. This is why you've dedicated your time to a worthy cause, so you can reap the rewards that come with your work.

～

"You gain strength, courage, and confidence by every experience in which you really stop to look fear in the face. You are able to say to yourself, 'I lived through this horror. I can take the next thing that comes along.'"
– Eleanor Roosevelt

～

Patches to the holes created by fear:

If you want to patch up the holes in your bucket list created by fear, follow these suggestions.

1. Know what you're dealing with. Identify your fears. List them. Name them. Expose them to the light. Sometimes just exposing them reduces the power they have over you. If this sounds familiar, it's because it's the same advice I gave for releasing shame in Chapter Two.

2. List the consequence to your life if you never did anything about these fears. Imagine it's the end of your life and you had never left your comfort zone, never took a risk, never asked for an opportunity, never raised your hand, never left the hurt behind. How would your life have turned out?

3. Make a decision. Action always starts with a decision. Decide that you want more for yourself. Decide that the courage to work through your fears is worth developing because of how you'll feel each time you check an item off your bucket list.

4. Step into the power of your dreams. Feel the excitement at the strength you are gaining just by making the decision to do more with your life.

5. Solicit help from others. Never underestimate the power of an accountability partner, a support team, or a mentor. Reach out to someone who will support you with encouragement and will celebrate with you at each milestone - large or small - on your journey.

6. The best way to overcome your fear is to do something that scares you. Once you feel the rush of doing something that you were afraid of doing, you'll have the confidence to try other things that scare you.

7. CELEBRATE! By all means, celebrate the overcoming of your fear - big time! You faced your fears and courageously moved ahead, despite them. You deserve all the joy, excitement, pleasure, and freedom, that comes from fulfilling your dreams. Congratulations!

Chapter 5 Wrap-Up:

1. Identify your fear
2. List the consequences of doing nothing
3. Make a decision
4. Step into your power
5. Solicit help
6. Do something that scares you
7. Celebrate!

Chapter 6
The DOUBT Hole

≈

"Be in doubt of your doubts and have faith in your faith"
- Pierre Goursat

≈

≈

"When in doubt, don't."
– Benjamin Franklin

≈

Chapter 6

The DOUBT Hole

Doubt will stop you in your tracks. Doubt produces the voices in your head that remind you of all the failed attempts in your past - or anybody's failure at anything, and makes you think that you'll probably fail, too. When you doubt your ability, or your strength, or your place in the world, it stops you from doing what you want to do. Doubt is like making up the ending to the movie before you see the opening title, and of course the ending to your movie is that you don't get the girl, you don't get the guy, you don't get the job, you don't win the race, you don't save the world; you fail miserably.

Since you've already decided you can't win, then why even bother to try? Sometimes we're in our own head so much that we talk ourselves out of what we're trying to do. We start out on the right path and then the doubt that we're making any progress sets in and we give up. "What's the use? This will never work. Here I go again. Another failure." Negative self-talk sabotages your drive and you lose hope of accomplishing whatever it was that you set out to do. Also, have you ever noticed that when you begin to doubt yourself, you start doubting others, too? It's as if the negativity of outcomes breeds more negativity.

If you have doubts or insecurities about achieving anything on your bucket list, you are not alone. If you look at actors, comedians, or athletes, you might see confident, accomplished people. You would think they have it all; fame, fortune, and opportunity, so they probably wouldn't relate to having doubt. Yet, many of them are plagued with insecurities and doubt. One of the best basketball players of all time, Kobe Bryant, said, *"I have self-doubt. I have insecurity. I have fear of failure. I have nights when I show up at the arena and I'm like, my back hurts, my feet hurt, my knees hurt. I don't have it. I just want to chill. We all have self-doubt. You don't deny it, but you also don't capitulate to it. You embrace it."*

Alanis Morissette sums doubt up well; *"Fame is hollow. It amplifies what is there. If there is any self-doubt, or hatred, or lack of ability to connect with people, fame will magnify it."*

Jennifer Lopez freely admits her thoughts on doubt, *"The biggest insecurity I had was my singing. Even though I had sold 70 million records, there was this feeling like, I'm not good at this."*

However, some people actually think doubt is *good*. That having doubt challenges you to always strive to be better, to not settle on your laurels; to push yourself further, to never say, "I've arrived." Ryan Reynolds is a famous actor who is married to the beautiful actress Blake Lively. He uses his insecurity. He says, *"Acting has given me a way to channel my angst. I feel like an overweight, pimply-faced kid a lot of the time - and finding a way to access that insecurity, and put it toward something creative is incredibly rewarding. I feel very lucky."*

If you can channel your self-doubt, great. The challenge is to not allow the self-doubt to grow into inactivity. It would be easy to doubt your way into paralysis, to take the safe way out and to never put yourself out there, never risk, so that you won't fail. On the other hand, you could be well on your way when the voice of doubt gets louder and louder, until it is no longer motivating you to do better, but convincing you to quit.

Take my friend Mark Jackson. The Denver Broncos drafted him in the 6th round. You would think that once he made it to training camp he would have all the confidence in the world, but doubt and insecurity set in and Mark decided that he probably wasn't good enough to make the team. He wanted to quit. During those tryouts, they had two practices a day, followed by team meetings. If you were late to *anything*, you could be fined $250. Mark made his decision to quit carefully, because he didn't have the $250 to pay the fine if he changed his mind. He packed all of his stuff before the 2nd practice, so that right after practice he could just shower and leave. He did just that. But when he got to the parking lot, there were some Bronco fans hanging out who noticed that Mark wasn't at practice. One guy even questioned him and knew that he would be fined if anyone caught him not in the meeting. Mark explained that he was quitting. "NO WAY!" The fan was astounded. "You can't quit! You're a Denver Bronco! Do you know how many people would give anything to just be in the position you're in right now?" The fan was so optimistic and so encouraging - emphatic, even - that Mark changed his mind. He turned around, went back to his room to drop off his suitcase, then went back to the meeting ready to face the consequences and pay the fine for being late. Strangely enough, that night there was a temporary power-outage which caused the team meeting to start late. No one even noticed that Mark had quit the team, changed his mind and came back.

Mark made the team. He went to the Super Bowl three times with the Denver Broncos. His career in the NFL lasted nine years. There is one final note to this story. The name of the fan in the parking lot was Mr. Angel. I always like to think that we have angels looking out for us when we have our doubts.

When doubt comes from your past experience:

If you've failed at something in the past, it would make sense that you would have some of the pain of that failure return if you attempt it again. More productively, you can take every experience, every attempt, and learn from it. What did you do right? What did you do wrong? What would you do differently? Your past doesn't need to dictate where your future ends up. Use your past as fuel, or as ammunition. Work toward going for it again, this time with more information. Keep building on the experience of your past attempts. That experience is priceless.

When doubt comes from other people:

Sometimes our doubt stems from being criticized by other people. Other people will doubt your ability, or your intention, or your skill. Break it down person by person Who is criticizing you? Who doubts you? Once you identify them, then ask yourself why the opinion of this person matters. Is this person close to you? Do they have your best interest in mind? Are they coming from a place of respect and honor? Are they simply giving you feedback? We can't go through life without being criticized, but that doesn't mean we have to credit everything we hear as being 100% true, then internalize it and allow our self-doubt to take over.

Is it unsolicited feedback?

If you are getting unsolicited feedback, chances are you may not be entirely prepared for it. When someone asks if you are open to feedback you might ask them to put it in writing, or maybe set up a specific time to discuss it, so that you're not totally caught off guard. If that's not possible - if they just come up and offer their opinion whether you want to hear it or not - then try to just listen to the facts. It can be so emotionally stressful to listen to criticism that we may not hear some valuable gems that could help us. If we're too defensive we may not hear *anything*. One way to not let emotions get in the way of a potentially awkward conversation is to ask questions. This is especially helpful when people just offer feedback with no warning at all. When they do, try gathering information first before you attach any emotion to what they're saying. "What do you mean?" "Can you give me an example?" Maybe even, "What would success look like?" Anything to keep them talking, so you can collect your thoughts. That way, you can formulate a response, even if it's only "Thank you for your feedback."

Is the feedback solicited?

If the feedback is solicited, then listen, even if the feedback isn't what you wanted to hear. Listen to it and look for the value in what's being offered. Get clear on what's being said. Ask good questions. Ask how you can improve. Be sure to thank them for taking the time to give you feedback, or for coaching or mentoring you. Then, if you want the relationship to continue, give them updates on what you've done with their feedback. Not all feedback will be right for you, so take what works and move on.

Giving and receiving feedback is never easy but, if done with grace, it gets easier. Knowing that it usually stings when we first hear it, but that it wears off and eventually helps us, will make it easier as well. When we get negative feedback, it's tempting to wallow in negativity and swim in the self-doubt that follows, but then it will be even more difficult to get back on track to fulfilling the dreams on your bucket list.

By the way, feedback can be encouraging and optimistic, too!

For that kind of feedback, you don't need my coaching. All I would add is that, when you hear kind, encouraging, hopeful words from friends, coaches, or mentors, by all means write them down in your win-list! Then when you have those moments of doubts you can pull them out and re-gain your confidence.

What about when you slip and start criticizing *yourself?* Where is that coming from? That doesn't serve any purpose at all. When you believe you were born to be a divine light shining in the world, why would you do anything to dim that light? How do you stop that criticizing voice in your head? One tip that I learned from the author and health-and-wellness coach, Angela Gaffney, may help you as well. She asked if I would ever use that same language I was using when I was feeding my self-doubt with criticsm, to that child? Probably not, as it may impact them in huge way, maybe even for life.

I thought of Stacy Sherman. She's my beautiful niece and grew up calling me Aunt Mandy. (It was our "thing" to have nicknames.) She's turned into such a wonderful young women and is now starting her career as a Delta Airlines flight attendant, crossing off her bucket-list items by seeing the wonders of the world. I'm so proud of her! Not for one second would I talk to her in the same way I talked to myself, in my darker moments. I love her too much for anyone to put her down and fill her head with such negativity! When I applied that little trick I got from Angela, I stopped with the self- criticism and negative thinking. It doesn't mean I'm 100% positive all the time, but I have no use for putting myself down anymore. Just like I wouldn't put up with anyone putting down Stacy.

Mistakes are going to happen. When we are putting ourselves out there and taking risks and trying new things, we will sometimes fail. Mistakes mean that we are trying, we are living and we're still in the game, not standing on the sidelines. Just make sure that when you make a mistake, you admit to it, and move on. It doesn't mean you were mistaken in trying, you just made a mistake in the execution. When we have that mindset, it's much easier to learn from criticism or feedback from others, whether it's solicited or not.

My final advice about overcoming doubt is that, after any attempt that doesn't go your way, you try again. Get moving again. The sooner you get back on the horse, so to speak, the less chance you have of getting stuck in wallowing in self-pity.

Patching the hole created by doubt:

The opposite of doubt is faith. Faith means having trust and/or confidence in something or someone unseen. When doubt starts to seep in, find a way to rest assured that things are going to work out, that things will be okay. On a practical level, remind yourself of how you got to where you are today. Look back on the hard work and perseverance it took to achieve the position you have. In essence, keep track of your wins as I suggested in a previous chapter and recall those wins when you have doubts. Remind yourself of your wins and have faith that you will continue to add wins to your list. You will continue to grow, to add value, to live an amazing life.

Also, it helps to occasionally get outside of your own head. When we have self-doubt, it's a sign that we need some encouragement from outside of ourselves. One way to get that is to go and look for signs of goodness in the world. Have you heard the phrase "My faith in humankind has been restored"? Usually people say this after reading about someone who performed an unselfish act, someone who displayed remarkable kindness and expected nothing in return. Those stories of hope and inspiration warm the heart and inspire you to do greater things; they put your own problems into perspective.

Do a quick search for inspiring stories and see what comes up. Ask people for the most inspiring story they've heard lately, then listen to the joy. For example, I recently had a speaking engagement in Bermuda and read up on the local flavor and culture. I didn't have to go far to discover a local hero named Johnny Barnes. While working at the Bermuda Railways, he would wave to people on his lunch hour. He noticed that this had such a positive affect on people. He decided after retiring, that he would stand out on a busy intersection and just wave at commuters and telling them, "I love you! God Bless you!" Rain or shine, Johnny A.K.A. Mr. Happy, would show up for hours every work day and wave at people. He became the ambassador for love and joy. Can you imagine? Before his death at age 93, they erected a life-size statue of him right where he spent, get this, almost 30 years waving at people.

Another example is Iraq War veteran Taylor Winston who became a hero because of his quick thinking during the horrific attack on concert goers in Las Vegas October 1, 2017. He said his military training helped him react quickly by finding a truck that he could immediately transport critically wounded people to the hospital. He was able to save lives that night by getting people aid when ambulances couldn't get there quick enough. His bravery was rewarded when a Gilbert, Arizona car dealership offered him a free truck of his own! B5 Motors went to social media with his picture saying "Please help us find this #Vegashero so we can give him a truck!" It didn't take long for people to find Taylor. I love stories like this where selfless acts are rewarded. Stories like these remind me of the goodness in the world. I believe our doubts can be squashed if we just make a shift in our mindset, to where we focus on faith and what we believe in and just relax. After all, what would be the alternative? Having no faith?

If having faith in *yourself* is too much of a stretch for you, then begin by being a supportive friend and being positive with others. Demonstrate optimism as opposed to doubt; show faith as opposed to being critical; show support instead of tearing down. Maybe you'll find that the positive energy you're giving out has a reciprocal effect and it will return back to you.

Finally, if you have spiritual faith, then you have an omnipotent force working for your good. Your doubts don't stand a chance when you turn your fears, concerns, and insecurities over to your God. It's not always easy to do, but that's what prayer and contemplation are for, to find strength and discernment. Many people turn to scripture to strengthen their faith. It's no coincidence that, "Be not afraid!" is mentioned 365 times in the Bible, in one form or another. Yes. Once a day, you can be reminded not to fear, but to have faith.

～

"Consult not your fears, but your hopes and your dreams. Think not about your frustrations, but about your unfulfilled potential. Concern yourself not with what you tried and failed in, but with what it is still possible for you to do."
–Pope John XXIII

～

Chapter 6 Wrap-Up:

1. You're not alone
2. Even famous people have doubt and insecurities
3. Use small doses of doubt as fuel
4. Analyze whoever is criticizing you
5. Ask questions to get clarity
6. Do not take feedback personally
7. Listen

8. Stop negative self-talk
9. Get back on the horse
10. Choose faith over doubt

Chapter 7
What if You're Stuck?

❧

"Inaction breeds doubt and fear. Action breeds confidence and courage. If you want to conquer fear, do not sit home and think about it. Go out and get busy."
– Dale Carnegie

❧

Chapter 7

What if You're Stuck?

At this point in the book, I hope you are terrifically inspired to write, or re-write , or cross things off of your bucket list. Just in case you get stuck and need a boost, let me help you get unstuck.

Get out of your own situation.

Just don't feed the homeless.

What?

Let me explain. Several years ago, my dear friends Tara and Mike Rayburn asked if my husband and I wanted to volunteer with a group of their friends to go feed the homeless for Thanksgiving. Yves, my husband, had run soup kitchens in France before he moved to the United States, so he was immediately on board with the idea. It was a pretty large group that came together, bringing turkeys with all the fixings, plenty to drink, table cloths, utensils, napkins; the whole deal. Everyone had a role, and mine was "greeter." It was a beautiful day in Las Vegas when we set up a bountiful spread in the park, near the streets where many of the homeless live. It was an incredibly rewarding day. Then, something happened on the way home that made me decide to never feed the homeless again; it's been about seven years and I never have. That something was a phone call from my sister on our way home. She had called me to wish me a Happy

Thanksgiving. During the call, she asked me what I did that day. I told her how fun it was to go and feed the homeless. Yves interrupted me while I was on the phone. He said something I'll never forget. He said, "Marilyn, you *feed* dogs and you *serve* the homeless."

That one line shifted my whole thinking. When you go from feeding to serving, you act differently. We now volunteer at Catholic Charities of Southern Nevada every Saturday that we are in town. They offer a free meal served every single day of the year so it is a joy for us to be able to choose Saturday as our day to serve. They have an early lunch meal from 10:00 am to 11:00 am to mostly men, but plenty of women too. When we show up for our shift, we never know what other volunteers we are going to see. Sometimes we see other regulars, and sometimes we meet new volunteers. Lots of the Las Vegas casinos do community service days and have their employees come down in groups to serve. Whoever shows up, I like to tell them we have a Saturday morning theme of the day. Our theme is "We serve with Joy and Dignity." What that means is when we say good morning and serve the folks their tray of food as they go through the line, we smile while we look them in the eye. The dignity part comes in when we have no expectation that they will say thank you. When you release expectation of other people's behavior, it makes it easier to serve with joy. Some of the homeless population are very happy to receive but are not as willing to smile. I'm in no position to judge, I'm just grateful that they are about to have a warm, well-balanced meal in a nice setting.

Why am I telling you this story, in the middle of this chapter about being unstuck? Because, no matter what my issues are throughout the week, no matter what frustrations I may have been experiencing, I always feel better after 11:00 am on Saturday, after serving lunch to between 300 to 600 people; people who, unlike myself, don't have a home to go to. My problems are so minuscule in comparison. If you want to get unstuck? Shift your perspective into gratitude.

I learned this lesson about gratitude when I was flying from Vegas to Atlanta with a layover in Dallas. My client was picking me up for dinner that night and I made a rookie travel mistake by wearing my cute shoes and not my comfy travel shoes. I walked awkwardly to my connecting flight. Halfway through the airport I realized I left my book on the plane. It was a great business book, too, so I hoofed it back to the arrival gate. The gate agent was very nice and went back on board and found my book and brought it to me. I walked to my connecting flight, relieved and happy, although my feet were really starting to hurt. I made it all the way to the new gate, only to discover that I had forgotten my purse at the first gate, when I was talking to the gate agent about retrieving my book. So off I went (again) running back to the first gate to claim my purse, hopefully before TSA confiscated it. Luckily, it was still there. Phew! Now that I had my book *and* my purse, my feet were done! So I bought some fuzzy socks at an airport convenience store and sat down, and that's when the self-pity began to settle in. You know what happens when you have a pity party - you invite guests. First, there's frustration, anxiety, and anger; they may be followed by resentment and stress. That's when you invite Ben and Jerry and maybe Jack! As I was rubbing my sore feet, I looked up and noticed a whole crowd of customers looking out the window. An eerie silence fell upon the terminal, so I asked a stranger standing next to me what everyone was doing. He pointed out the window and that's when I saw it: An American Airlines flight loading a luggage cart that had an American flag draped over it. Eight or nine members of the ground crew had run to salute what turned out to be a casket of a fallen soldier as it was moving up the conveyer belt into the cargo hold of the plane. It was a deeply moving sight, with so many strangers showing such reverence for a fallen soldier they didn't even know. While I watched this scene unfold, I was overcome with gratitude. I was grateful for the crew and my fellow passengers, but mostly I was grateful for the sacrifice made by this unknown soldier. I don't know how the soldier died. I don't even know if it was a man or a women. All I know is that my perspective shifted that day. I thought, who am I to complain because my feet hurt, or for struggling to make a connecting flight, when I'm witnessing someone's final flight home. Immersed in sorrow and gratitude, I no longer had pain in my feet.

Then it hit me.

You can't walk in gratitude and sit in self-pity at the same time.

If you are stuck in self-pity, find a way to get into gratitude. By the way, you can replace self-pity in this sentence with *anything* that doesn't serve you; you can't walk in gratitude and sit in *anger* at the same time; or *frustration*, or *anxiety*.

How do you find gratitude? Look for it. Create a journal to collect things for which you're grateful. A beautiful sunset. A warm exchange with a stranger. A compliment from someone you admire. Imagine, if you added something to your gratitude list every day for a week or 10 days, you would begin to notice more and more things to be grateful for. You can even take it a step further.

To celebrate my husband Yves' birthday, I decided take an idea from a book I read by Darren Hardy called, *The Compound Effect*. Mr. Hardy wrote a letter to his wife every day, then gave them all to her on Thanksgiving. I loved this idea and I tried it myself. I bought a blank journal and every day for a year I wrote a love letter to Yves (my Frenchie). Each night, while he was reading, I wrote in this journal. He thought I was writing in my diary. He knows that my diary is off limits, so he was never even tempted to look in it. If he did, he would have seen letters of love, lists of reasons I was glad we were married, recollections of moments of our day, all captured in this journal for him. Here's what was so cool about doing this journal for him: I started it as a birthday gift for him, but it ended up being a gift for both of us. You see, occasionally he would get on my nerves in the morning. When I noticed how annoyed I was, my brain would kick in and remind me that I had to write a love letter to him that night! You know, when you write someone a love letter, you never write anything that annoys you, you only write things that you love about them. My resilience was much stronger. Meaning, I bounced back from annoyance to love much quicker. Because I bounced back quicker to love, he bounced back quicker as well. Yves said it was the best gift he had ever received, he called it priceless. The fun, unexpected part of this process was that I didn't know how he was going to read it. Would he read it all in one setting? Would he break it up and read part of it at a time? He decided to read one day at a time, and he read it out loud. By reading it that way, we were reminded of how special our days together were. It was as if we re-lived all the best part of our previous year together.

When I ask my audience members if they would rather have a book of love letters or an expensive present, they overwhelmingly respond by saying they'd rather have the journal. I had a guy who wanted me to sell journals along with my motivational books. I told him I do offer journals. He said "Can you sell them pre-populated?" I thought that was hilarious. The good news is, you don't have to do it for a whole year. Try it for a just a week, or a month. It will get you unstuck.

Here are some other ideas to get back on track:

- Go inward and think about what you really want
- Focus on one thing at a time and don't overwhelm yourself
- Re-commit than focus on what's most important to you
- Allow yourself a limited time to complain and cry, then get back on track
- Get outside - commune with nature
- Listen to great music
- Mediate
- Pray
- Write
- Read inspirational writings
- Therapy
- Accepting that where you are is where you're supposed to be
- Every day is an opportunity to start over
- Go ice climbing (My friend Margo Talbot is an ice climber - she finds so much joy and peace in climbing frozen waterfalls. This may not be for everyone!)
- Go hiking
- Go for a walk
- Call a friend
- Ask for help
- Re-read this book!

My friend John Polish was undoubtedly stuck. He and his wife experienced the unimaginable loss of a baby, then their relationship ended in divorce. His life's work is now helping people get unstuck. He's so committed, he even started something called, "The Unstuck Happiness Conference." He has on his bucket list to hold a conference in all 50 states. One of the ways he suggests we get unstuck is to stop asking, "Why me?" and focus instead on, "What is it that I'm supposed to learn from this?" He says:

"When we get stuck it is very difficult to see past our own circumstances. It's easy to lose hope. No matter what adversity you are facing, if you are willing to pick yourself up and move forward there are opportunities waiting for you but they will never meet you in the middle of the wreckage. Those first few steps will not be easy. That is why I created Unstuck Happiness Conferences, to help people see that it is possible to find happiness, even after tragedy."

Final Bucket List Twist

Just when I was completing this book, I met a woman named Chérie Roe, and she had a different view of her bucket list that I think would be of tremendous value to you.

As long as she could remember, she loved playing the piano. She begged for lessons as early as five years old. She had a photo of Carnegie Hall on her wall like I would have photos of Elton John on mine (I grew up in the 70's!). Finally at eight years old, she was granted lessons and immediately showed talent. She collected applications and brochures to the world-renowned music school Julliard in New York City.

Although she was dedicated and committed to playing the piano, her dad tried to talk her out of making any career out of music. Fear and doubt set in and she thought to herself, "Who am I to apply to Julliard? What makes me think that I'm so special?" She put away those brochures and instead, she applied and attended a small college on a full scholarship. She let the 'Be safe, marry a doctor' message seep into her mindset and she stopped her dreams of performing live. She got married, had a baby and thought that's what her life was supposed to be. But, something kept nagging at her. She went to a program sponsored by her church called, "Become A Life Virtuoso" taught by my friend Mike Rayburn, who I mentioned earlier (http://mikerayburn.com). She learned two things from the course that became her turning point:

1. Forgive yourself for past mistakes and prior choices you've made. When she did this, she stopped beating herself up for not applying to Julliard.

2. She wrote down what was in the deepest part of her heart. What would she do if she permitted herself to really live her life?

That's when she made the decision.

She decided, "I'm going to apply to Julliard – just to take it off of my bucket list!"

I love that answer. It had been on her list since she was a little girl. She spent a lifetime denying herself, distracting herself, and living a good life, but not the ultimate fulfilling life. Her belief at the time was she would apply so she no longer would have that 'What if...' thought in her head. She never thought she would get in because Julliard is one of the most prestigious music schools in the world with the acceptance rate of less than 8%.

When Chérie applied, she made it through the first round, and that was good enough for her. When she made the cut for a live audition, she was thrilled to perform live once again. And, she would be satisfied with making it that far. Well, Chérie was accepted, and her very supportive husband moved her and their little girl to NYC for her to pursue her dream. She would never have this amazing life if she had left it un-pursued on her bucket list.

What is still on your list that you could just try, even if you don't believe yet that it will come true? What can you do so you can just take it off of your list? Worse case scenario is, it doesn't work out. The best-case scenario is it does!

Thank you, Mike and Tara, for inviting Frenchie and me to witness the concert at your home with Chérie and world-famous cellist Khari Joyner. Chérie had no idea I was writing a book on Bucket Lists when, after her show, I asked, "How did you get from Las Vegas to apply to Julliard?" That's when she said, "I applied just to get it off of my bucket list."

Chapter 7 Wrap-Up:

I hope that you are encouraged to go beyond what you think is possible, to dream bigger than you have ever dreamed before, to impact more lives than you ever imagined you could. Imagine the excitement, joy, hope, and exhilaration, you feel when you accomplish something you've set out to do. Imagine the sense of, "I did it" when you conquered your fear and crossed something off of your list. That's the energy in which I hope you bring to your day, week, month, year. I want you to swim in the energy of positive emotion as it washes over you and catapults you out of any fear and doubt and into your next challenge. With every item you cross off your bucket list, I hope the confidence that grows in you, gives you the momentum to write even more things on your list. I hope that your bucket list remains ongoing, so you have something to look forward to each and every day.

1. Shift your perspective
2. Start a gratitude journal
3. Be of service
4. Decide to be unstuck
5. Forgive yourself for past decisions

Chapter 8

Bucket Lists

Chapter 8
Bucket Lists

Now is your chance to create the life of your dreams. Use these as guidelines for creating your own bucket lists for different areas of your life.

I've given you lots of pages to write out whatever you want. The last one is for your ULTIMATE bucket list, the one where perhaps you can prioritize the things you would want from each of the categorized lists. I suggest too, that each time you pick up this book to write in any of these bucket lists, put a date by your notes. Then, put a reminder for 6 months from now, or every year on a certain date to check your list. Don't forget to remind yourself where you put this book!

As I write this book, friends of mine were giving me examples from their own bucket lists. Some were long, some were only about travel, but none surprised me more than Manley Feinberg's list. His list was very short. It only had two things on it, and they were very creative. Manley said:

"I have an extremely short bucket list, only two items. It was just one item until this summer. It's short because most of what I think might be "bucket list items" for most people, I'm not willing to wait to do. I have crazy dreams that crop up, and then I try to make them

happen, and most often some form of the dream comes to be. That one item for me has been to live in Yosemite National Park for one full year, while being deeply present with the beauty of the place and all the seasons in sequence, while reading and contemplating John Muir's, "The Yosemite" every single day. That's it, my only bucket list items for about 24 years now until this summer, when I added #2 which is to live on a sailboat for one full year based in the Caribbean."

There are no right or wrong answers to creating or living your bucket list. This book was meant to help you patch any holes that may prevent you from having the items on your bucket list come true. I hope that I have helped you accomplish that.

I firmly believe that when you are living out your dreams, you can't help but inspire others to live out theirs. In this day and age, we could *all* stand to live in a more inspired world. Here's to your success!

My Travel Bucket List

_____

_____

_____

_____

_____

_____

_____

_____

_____

_____

_____

_____

_____

_____

_____

_____

_____

_____

_____

_____

My Family Bucket List

_____

_____

_____

_____

_____

_____

_____

_____

_____

_____

_____

_____

_____

_____

_____

_____

_____

_____

_____

_____

My Physical Bucket List

_____

_____

_____

_____

_____

_____

_____

_____

_____

_____

_____

_____

_____

_____

_____

_____

_____

_____

_____

_____

_____

My Financial Bucket List

_____

_____

_____

_____

_____

_____

_____

_____

_____

_____

_____

_____

_____

_____

_____

_____

_____

_____

_____

_____

_____

_____

_____

_____

My Philanthropic Bucket List

_____

_____

_____

_____

_____

_____

_____

_____

_____

_____

_____

_____

_____

_____

_____

_____

_____

_____

_____

My Friendship Bucket List

My Professional Work Bucket List

_____

_____

_____

_____

_____

_____

_____

_____

_____

_____

_____

_____

_____

_____

_____

_____

_____

_____

_____

My Relationship Bucket List

_____

_____

_____

_____

_____

_____

_____

_____

_____

_____

_____

_____

_____

_____

_____

_____

_____

_____

_____

_____

_____

_____

My Ultimate Bucket List

_____

_____

_____

_____

_____

_____

_____

_____

_____

_____

_____

_____

_____

_____

_____

_____

_____

_____

_____

_____

About Marilyn

Marilyn Sherman has spent the last 22 years as a professional speaker, inspiring audiences of all sizes to get out of their comfort zone and get a front-row seat in life. She has a passion for helping people live the life of their dreams. She has been named one of the top 10 Motivational Keynote Speakers in the United States, and one of the Top Ten Female Speakers for Women's Conferences. She also is a finalist for top speakers in Las Vegas. One of the things Marilyn crossed off her relationship bucket list was to meet a man who spoke French. In 2005, she married Yves de Boisredon who moved from Paris, France to San Diego, California. After meeting in San Diego, they moved to Las Vegas where they currently reside. One of her Bucket List items left to fulfill is to host groups in France where she can share her love for the French countryside while visiting friends and family along the way.

Other books by Marilyn Sherman:

Whose Comfort Zone Are You In? How to lead the life you want and be happy every day.

Why Settle for the Balcony? How to get a Front-row Seat in Life.

Front-Row Service

For speaking availability, please contact her office at *info@marilynsherman.com* or visit her website at *www. MarilynSherman.com.*

Made in the USA
Columbia, SC
09 March 2019